Belwin Comprehensive Band Method

correlating **Individual Instruction** with **Group Instruction**

by Frank Erickson

in collaboration with:

Sue Collado
Richard J. Langen
Carol Pelkner
Eleanor Tibbals

Featuring:

Two Methods in One - Part 1 for individual or like instrument instruction and Part 2 for band class instruction.

Harmony from the Start - The band section is harmonized from the beginning.

Ranges - Each instrument is kept in its **easiest playing range** in **both** the individual and band sections.

Rhythm - Book 1 teaches rhythm only through **quarter notes** (except Percussion, which includes eighth notes). Move on quickly to Book 2.

Band Numbers - Book 1 includes seven performance pieces suitable for programming.

Instrumentation

Conductor	F Horn
Flute	Trombone
Oboe	Baritone B.C.
Bassoon	Baritone T.C.
Bb Clarinet	BBb Tuba
Bb Bass Clarinet	Timpani
Eb Alto Saxophone	Bells (Mallet Percussion)
Bb Tenor Saxophone	Percussion (Snare Drum,
Eb Baritone Saxophone	Bass Drum and
Bb Trumpet	Auxiliary Percussion)

Cover Design/Photography: Warren E. Conway
Illustrations: Raine Clotfelter

NOTES

FINGERING CHART

TRUMPET

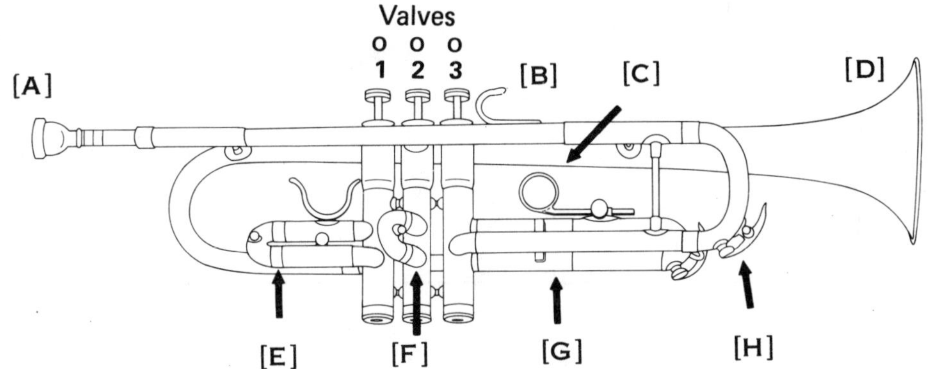

● - means valve down
o - means valve up

When two notes are given together on the chart (F♯ and G♭ as an example), they sound the same and are played with the same fingering.

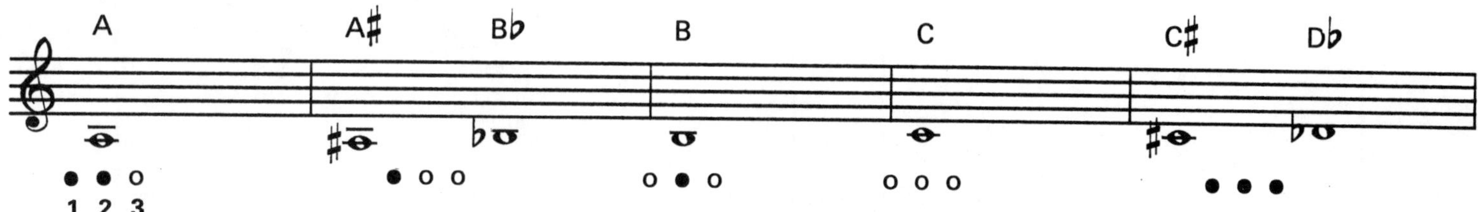

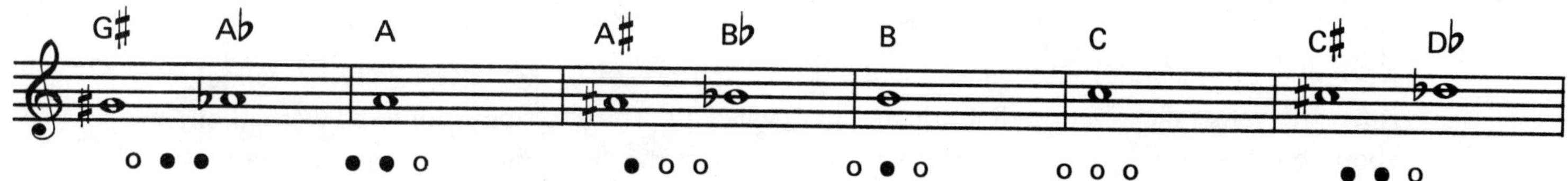

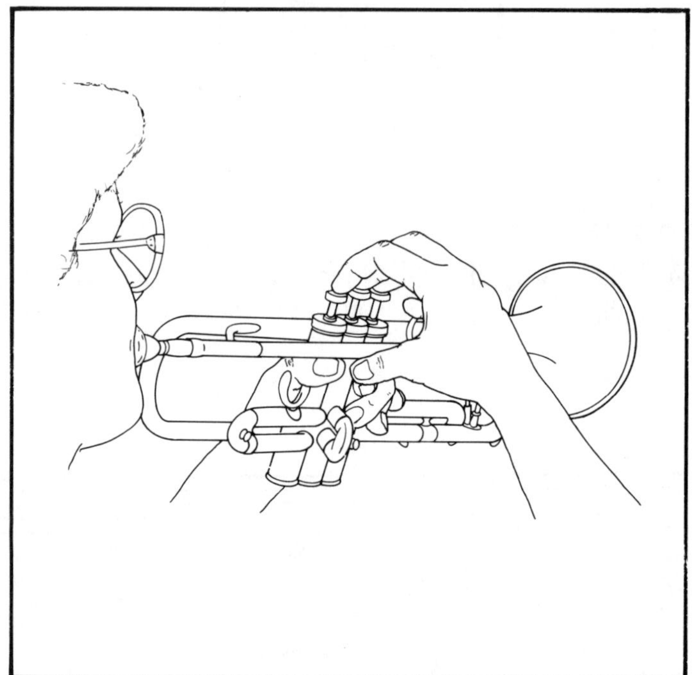

The Trumpet is held by the left hand with the fingers placed around the valve casings. The little finger of the right hand is placed on <u>top</u> of the "Pinky" ring. Push the valves down hard and straight. The fingers are curved and rest on the valves between the finger tip and the pad of the first joint. The left wrist should be straight.

Keep the tuning slides clean and greased with slide grease or petroleum jelly (Vaseline). Keep the valves clean and well lubricated with valve oil. The Trumpet should be washed out about once a week by running warm water through the instrument, starting at the bell. About once a month it should be taken apart and thoroughly cleaned with warm soapy water. The mouthpiece should be cleaned regularly with the mouthpiece brush.

Caution should be used when laying the instrument down: make sure the first and second valve slides are facing up. If your mouthpiece should become stuck, use a mouthpiece puller, never a pair of pliers.

FUNDAMENTALS

STAFF

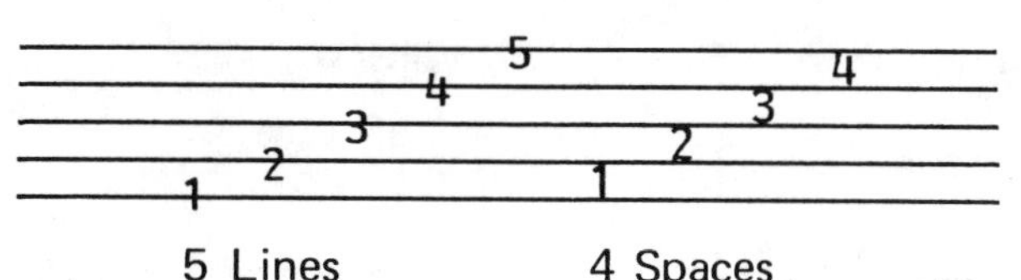

5 Lines   4 Spaces

TREBLE CLEF

BAR LINE

ONE MEASURE

DOUBLE BAR

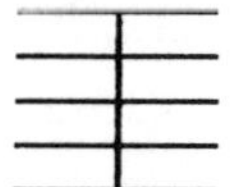
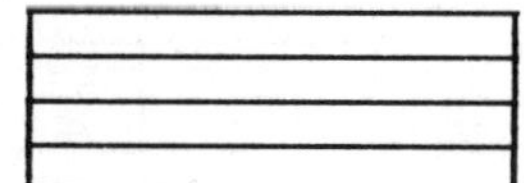
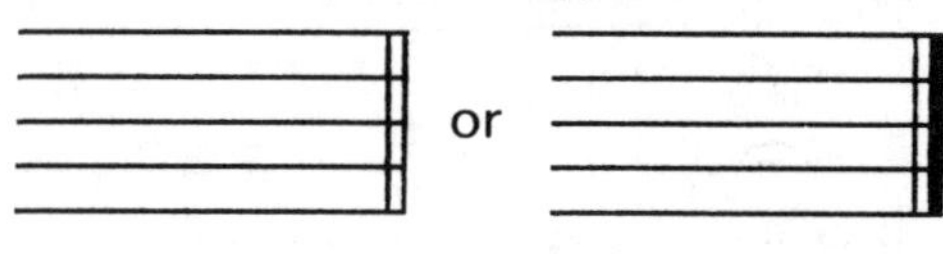

End of section.   End of number.

PIANO KEYBOARD

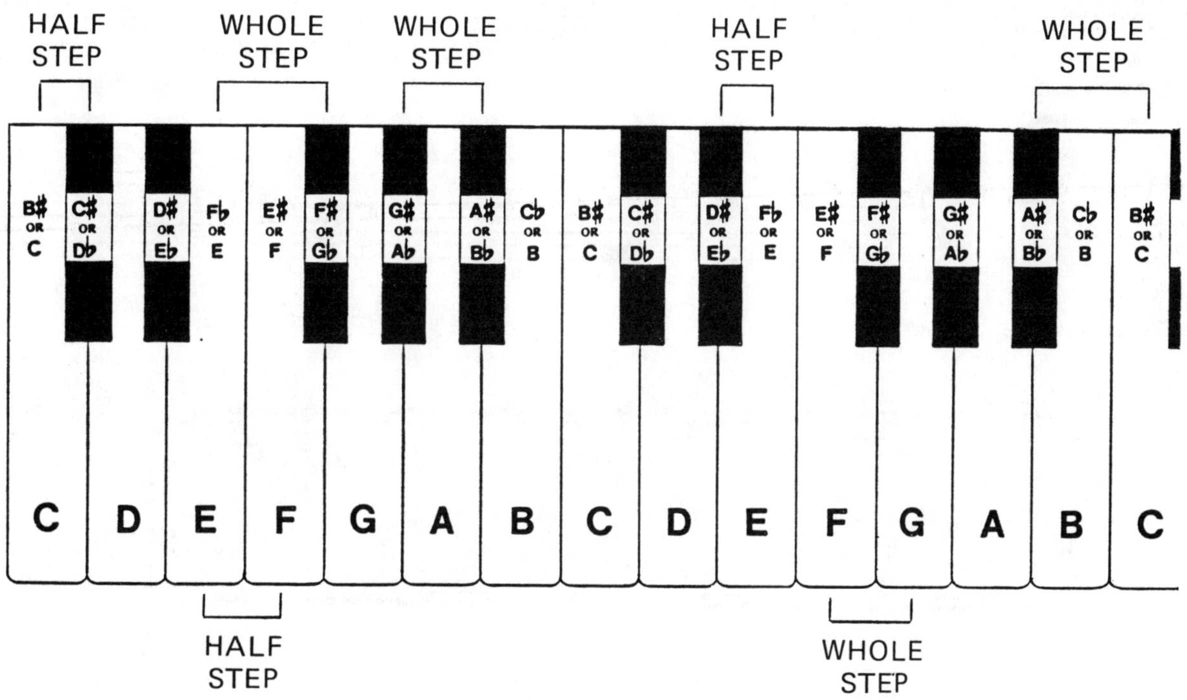

HALF STEP

The distance between any two adjoining notes whether they are black or white keys.

WHOLE STEP

Two half steps = one whole step.

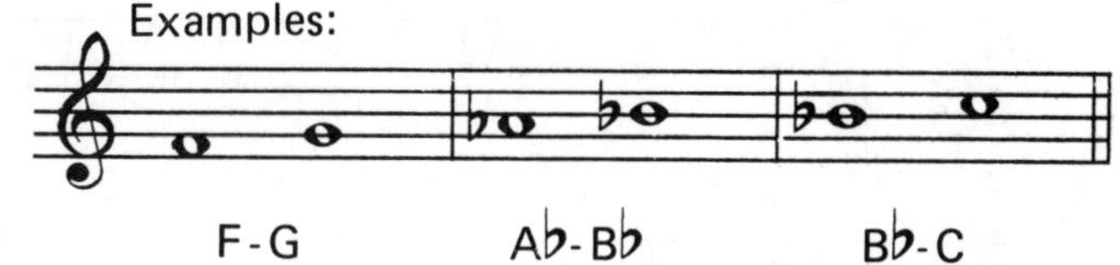

UNIT 1

Some teachers prefer to start with quarter notes rather than whole notes. If this is preferred, you may start with Examples 4 - 6 and follow with Examples 1 - 3.

TIME SIGNATURE

4/4 — 4 beats in each measure. Quarter note (♩) gets 1 beat.

WHOLE NOTE

𝅝 gets 4 beats.

WHOLE REST

Rest the entire measure.

In 4/4 Time the Whole Rest gets 4 beats.

1

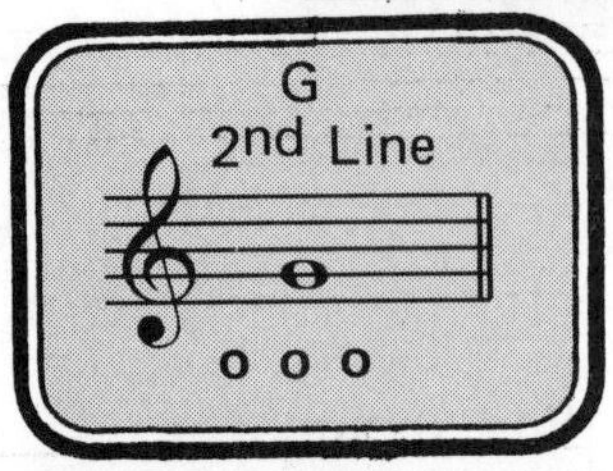
G
2nd Line

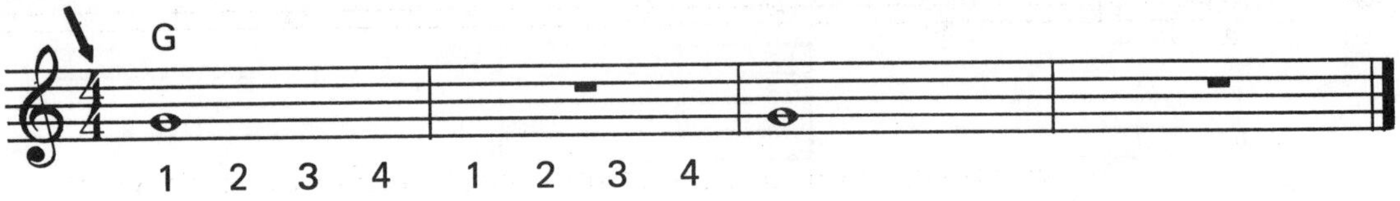
G
1 2 3 4 1 2 3 4

2

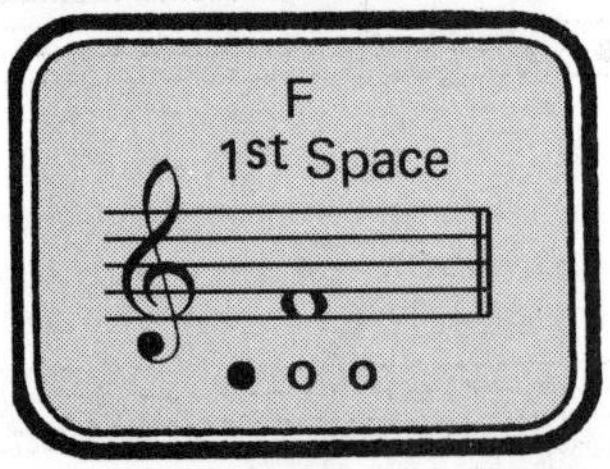
F
1st Space

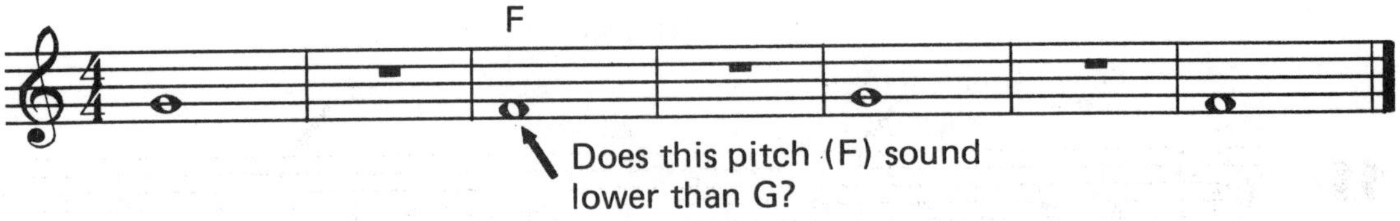
F
Does this pitch (F) sound lower than G?

3

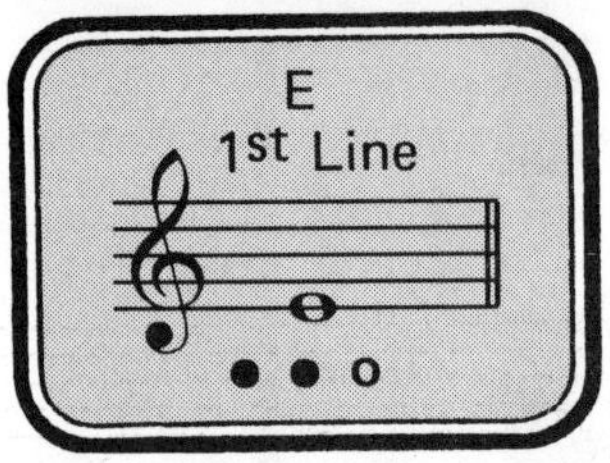
E
1st Line

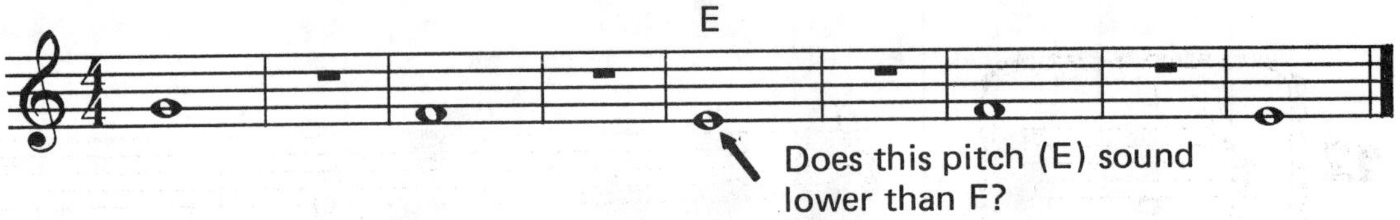
E
Does this pitch (E) sound lower than F?

QUARTER NOTE

In 4/4 Time ⇨ ♩ gets 1 beat.

QUARTER REST

𝄽 gets 1 beat.

Try to play four notes in one <u>continuous</u> breath. Do not stop the air when tonguing. Play slowly enough to get a good tone on each note.

4

1 2 3 4 1 2 3 4

5

1 2 3 4

6

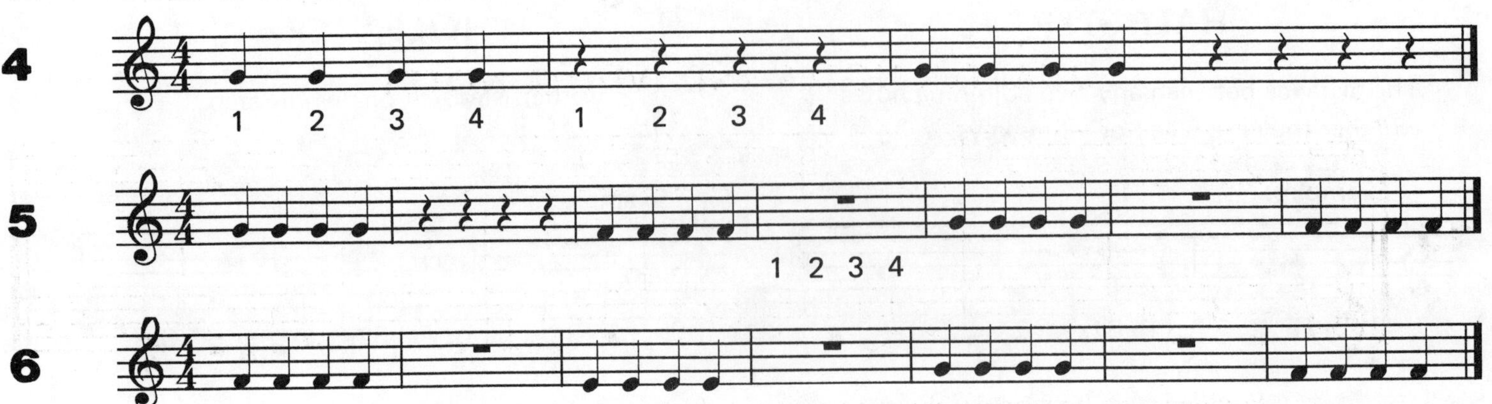

Practice each line separately, then play as a duet.

UNIT 2

In 4/4 Time
HALF NOTE
gets 2 beats.
HALF REST
gets 2 beats.
1
1 2 3 4
2
1 2 3 4
3
When breathing, do not take the mouthpiece off your lips.
Take air in through the corners of your mouth.
4
5
1 2 3 4
Ledger Line - A short added line above or below the staff.
C
6
Common Time (C) - Same as 4/4
7
1 2 3 4
Name these notes and try to sing them.
SOME WIDE SKIPS
8
MERRILY WE ROLL ALONG
(Melody)
9

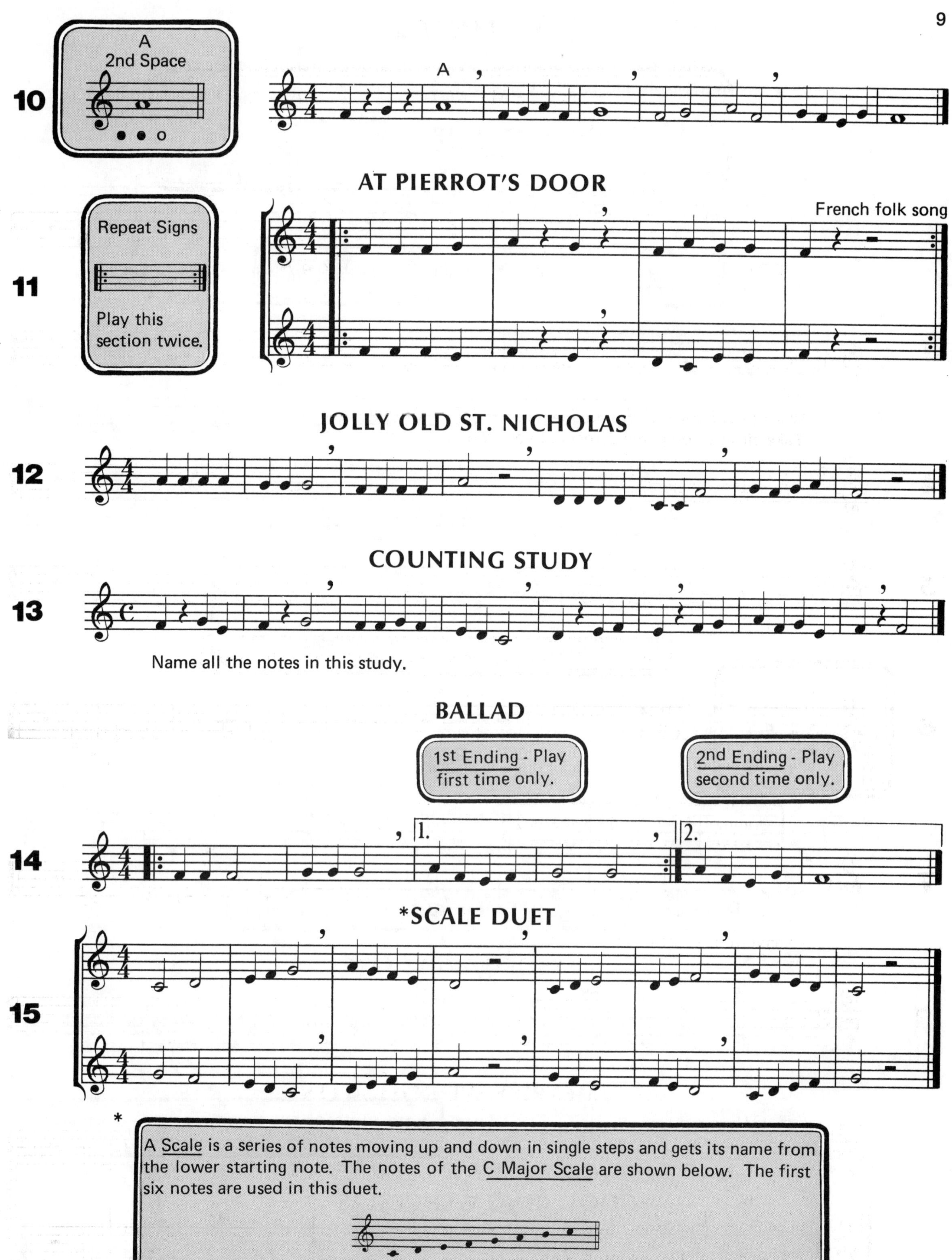
A
2nd Space
10
Repeat Signs
Play this section twice.
11
A
AT PIERROT'S DOOR
French folk song
JOLLY OLD ST. NICHOLAS
12
COUNTING STUDY
13
Name all the notes in this study.
BALLAD
1st Ending - Play first time only.
2nd Ending - Play second time only.
1.
2.
14
*SCALE DUET
15
* A Scale is a series of notes moving up and down in single steps and gets its name from the lower starting note. The notes of the C Major Scale are shown below. The first six notes are used in this duet.
C D E F G A B C

UNIT 3

It is important that each time you practice you begin with a warm-up exercise. It should be played slowly and quietly, unless otherwise indicated.

WARM-UP

A <u>Tie</u> joins and combines the value of two or more notes. Tongue the first note only.

Hold 3 beats.   Hold 5 beats.

OH SUSANNA

8

1. / 2.

1 2 3 4

A <u>Tie</u> carries an accidental into the next measure.

All F#'s

THE TROUBADOUR

English folk song

9

1. / 2.

Name all the notes in this number.

(F#)

WEST BOUND TRAIN

Western folk song

10

TWO PIECES BY BELA BARTOK
I. Shepherd's Dance

11

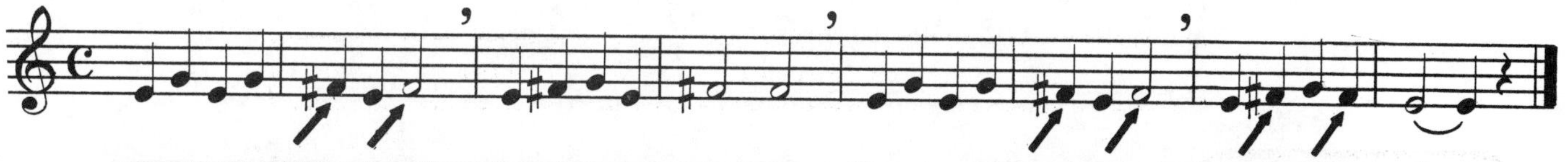

All of these notes are F#. An accidental remains in effect throughout the measure. Intervening notes do not affect this rule.

II. *Etude

12

*<u>Etude</u> (pronounced "Ātude") - A French term for a musical <u>study</u> or <u>exercise</u>.

UNIT 4

WARM-UP

1
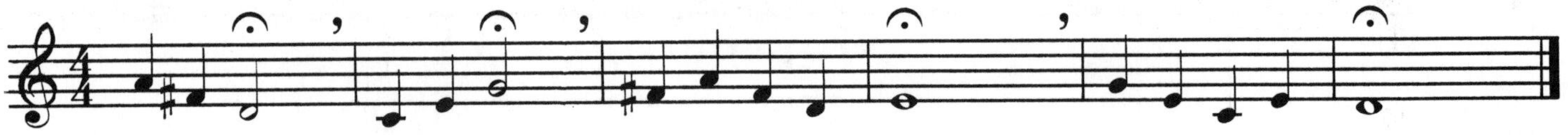

In $\frac{3}{4}$ Time - 3 beats in each measure.

2
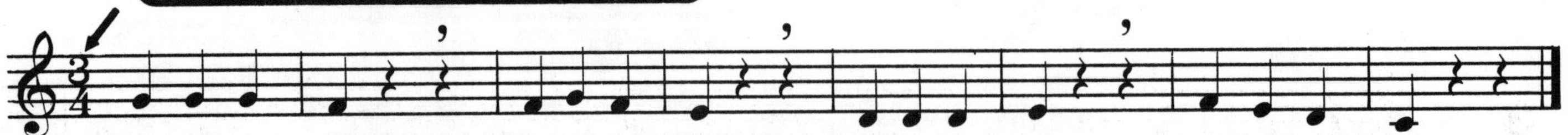
1 2 3 1 2 3

A Dot adds one half to a note's value.
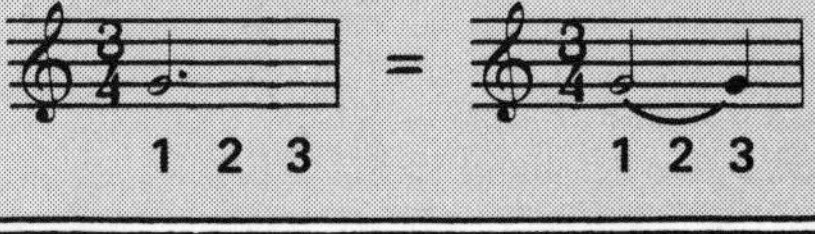
=
1 2 3
1 2 3

3
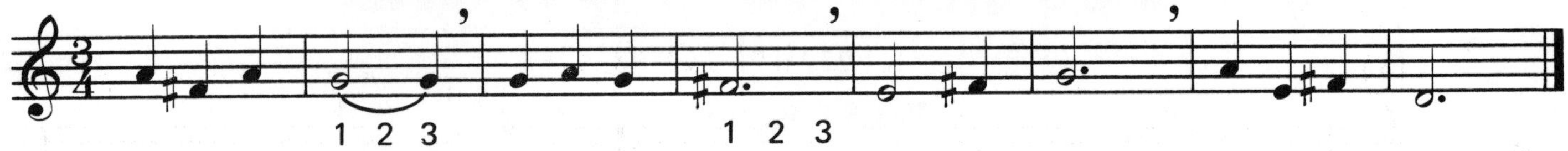
1 2 3
1 2 3

A Flat (♭) is an accidental that lowers a note one half step.

B♭
3rd Line
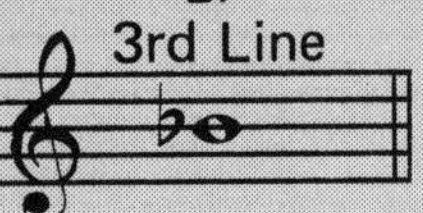
● o o

4
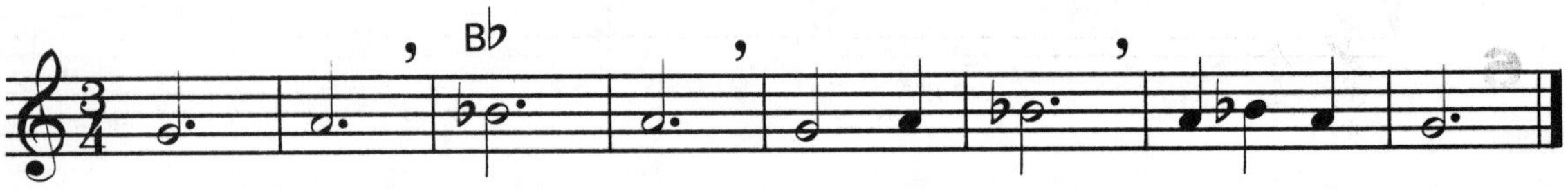
B♭

WHOLE REST
Rest the entire measure.
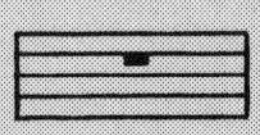
1 2 3
In $\frac{3}{4}$ Time the Whole Rest gets 3 beats.

5
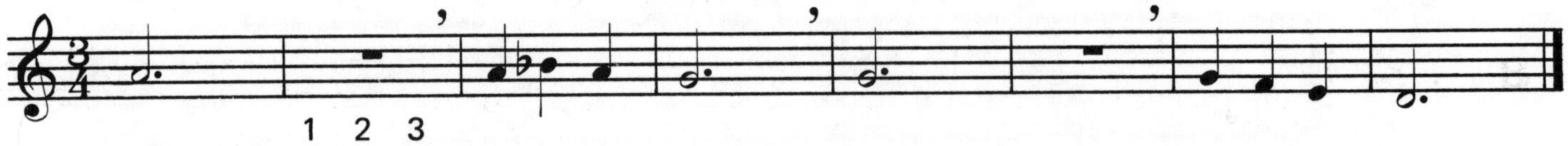
1 2 3

POP GOES THE WEASEL

6

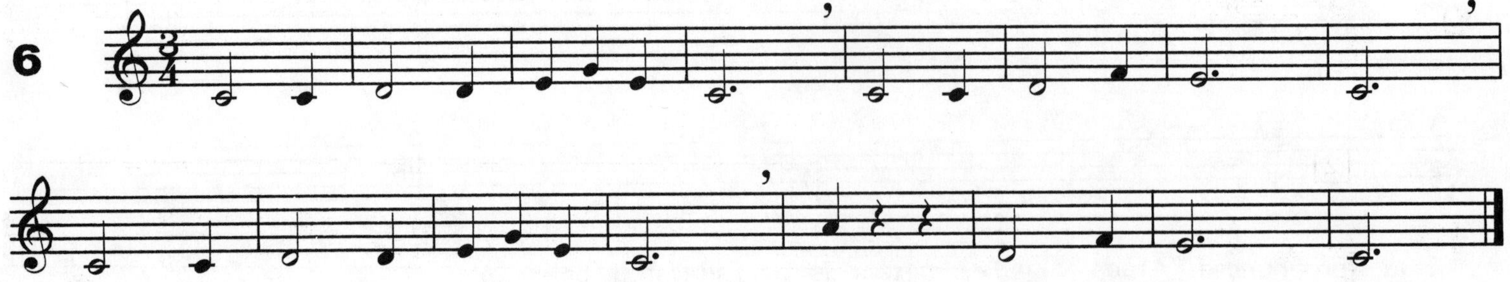

DUET WITH SKIPS

FAITH OF OUR FATHERS

UNIT 5

Play the notes connected with a <u>Slur</u> (⌢ or ⌣) smoothly and tongue the first note only.

WARM-UPS

F MAJOR SCALE STUDY

9

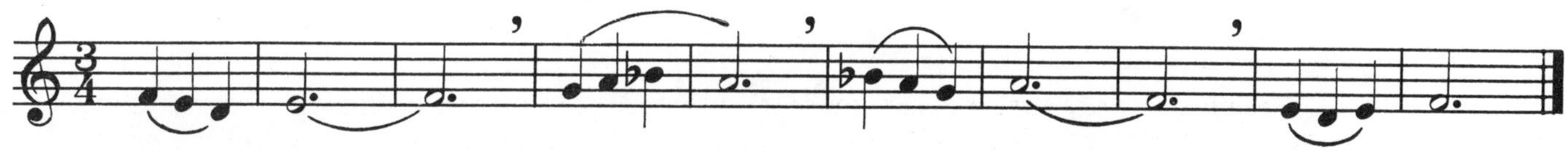

> ### THE KEY OF F MAJOR
> In the previous exercise it was necessary to add a flat before each B. To simplify this it will now be written in another way. B♭ is added at the beginning. This is the Key Signature of F Major. It means that all B's, in any octave, are played as B♭. These are the notes of the F Major Scale:
>
> **F G A B♭ C D E F** 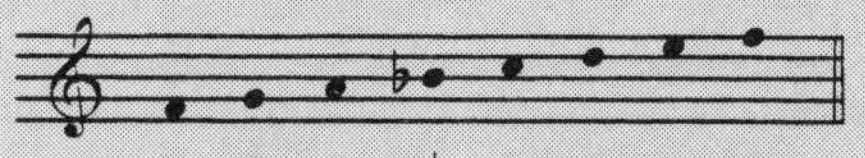

Key Signature of F Major

10

(B♭)

FIGHT THE GOOD FIGHT

Hymn Tune

11

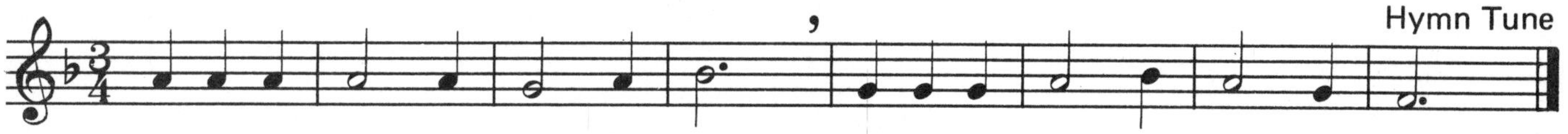

CHORALE THEME

Richard *Wagner

12

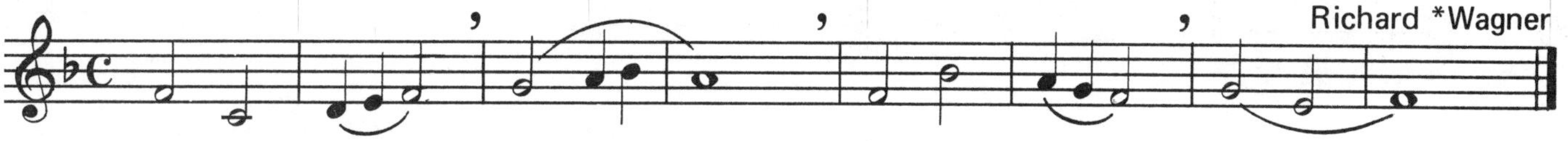

*Pronounced "Vogner"

> ### THE KEY OF C MAJOR
> In the Key of C Major there is No Key Signature - All notes are natural. These are the notes of the C Major Scale: 
>
> **C D E F G A B C**

SCHERZO IN C MAJOR

(Melody)

13

(Melody)

C MAJOR ARTICULATION STUDY

14

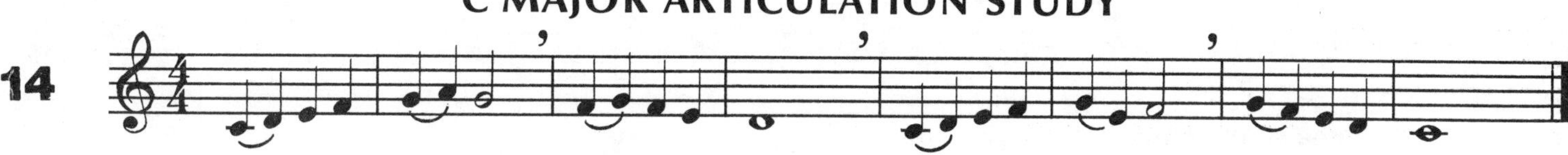

UNIT 6

WARM-UP

Name all the notes in these two studies.

In a <u>Round</u>, both players play the same melody, but the second player doesn't start until the first player reaches ②. At that point the second player starts at the beginning.

FIRST ROUND

This round is played like this:

MINUET

Louis Marchand

There are two <u>Pick-Up Notes</u> in the following number. The repeat also begins on the 3rd beat.

MARINE'S HYMN

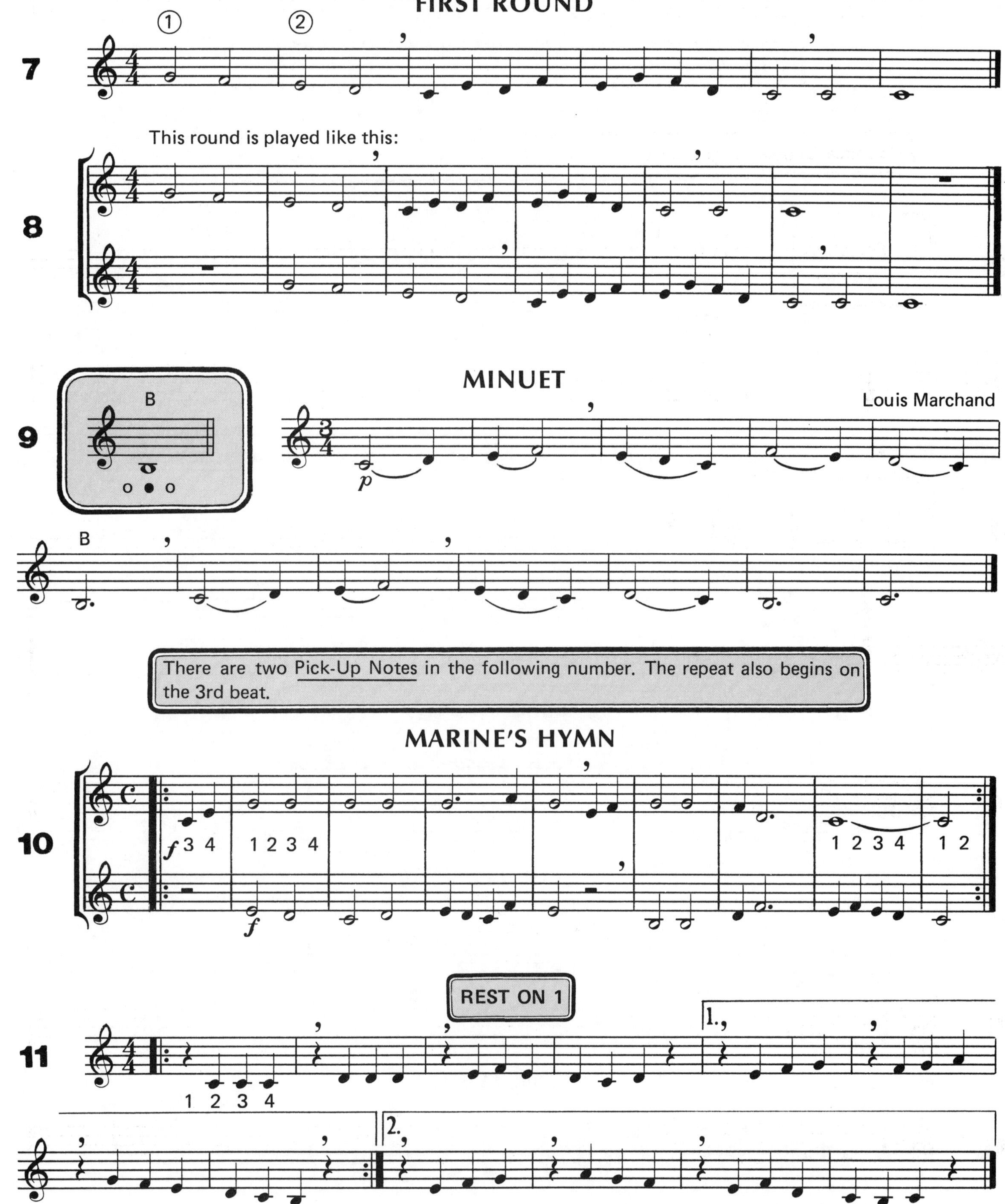

UNIT 7

WARM-UP

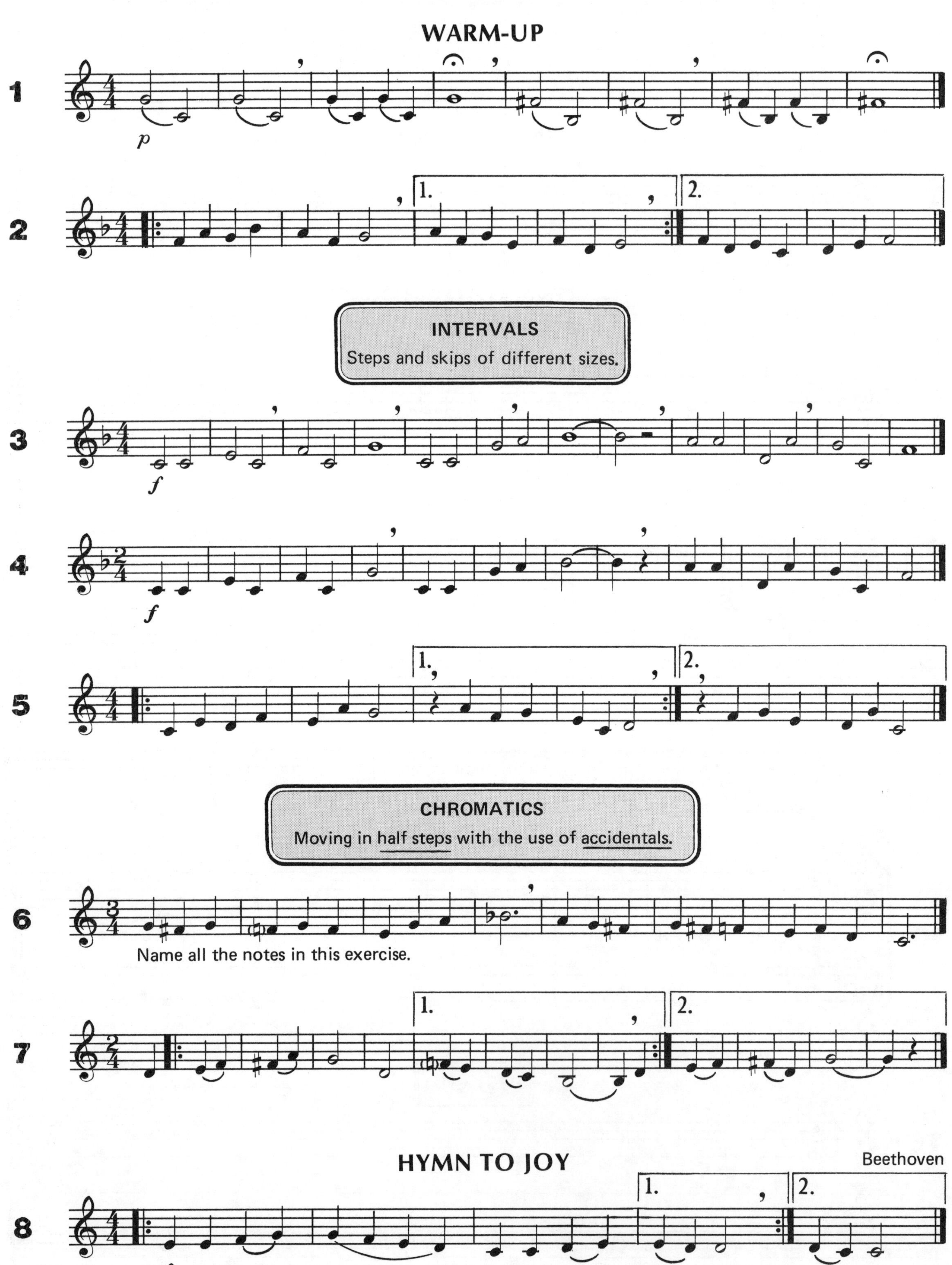

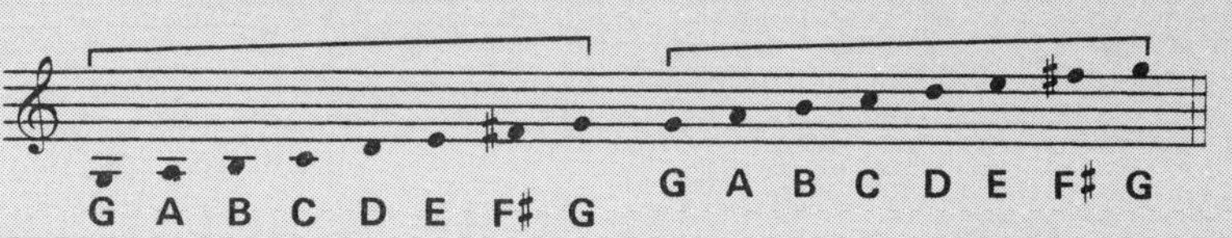

THE KEY OF G MAJOR

''The Song of the Princess'' is written in the Key of G Major. In this key an F♯ is placed in the Key Signature and all F's are played as F♯. Although the F♯ in the key signature is placed on the top line of the staff, it applies to any octave. These are the notes of the G Major Scale, shown in two octaves:

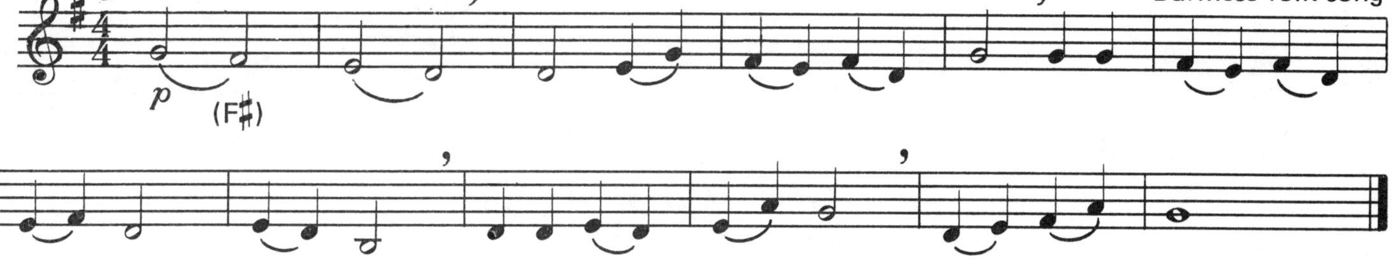

THE SONG OF THE PRINCESS

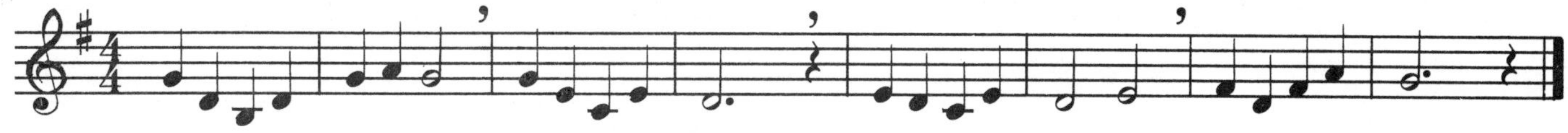

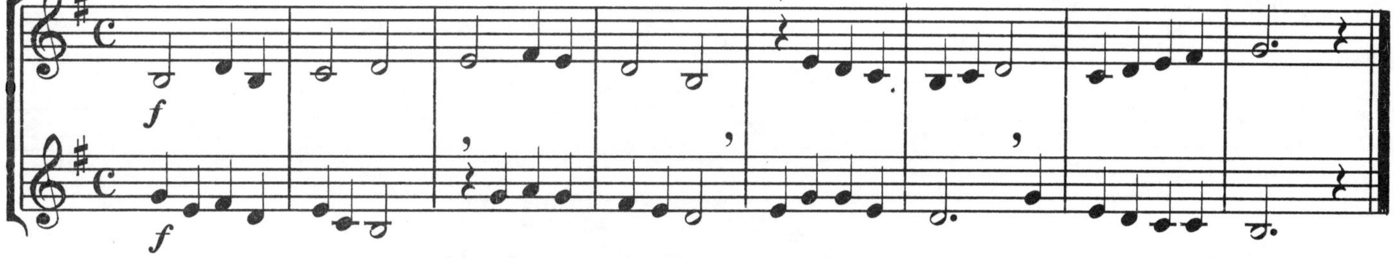

THE PIPER

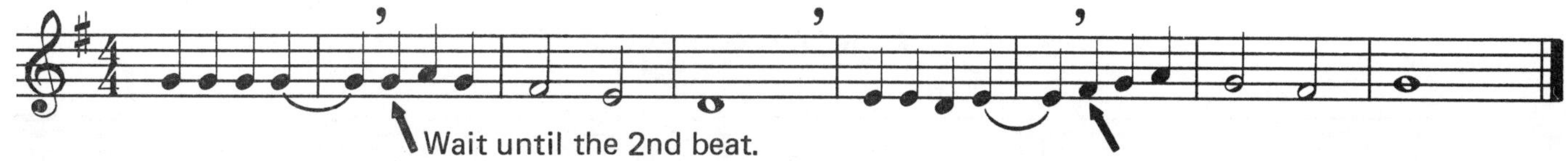

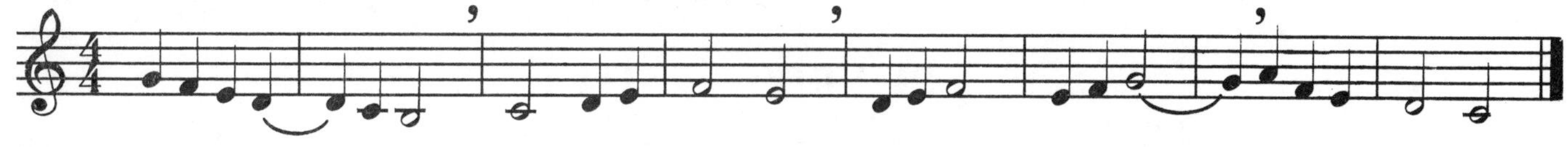

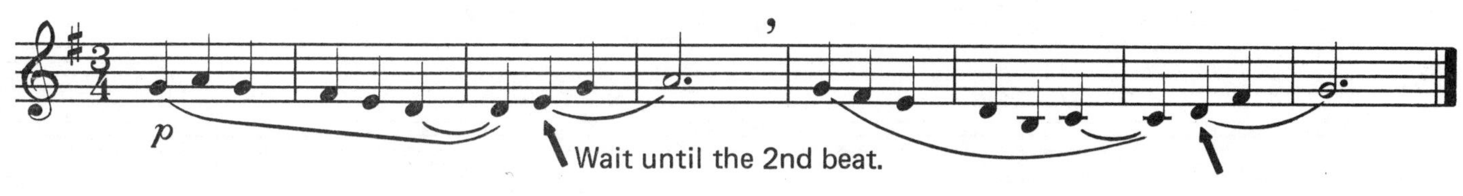

UNIT 8

WARM-UP

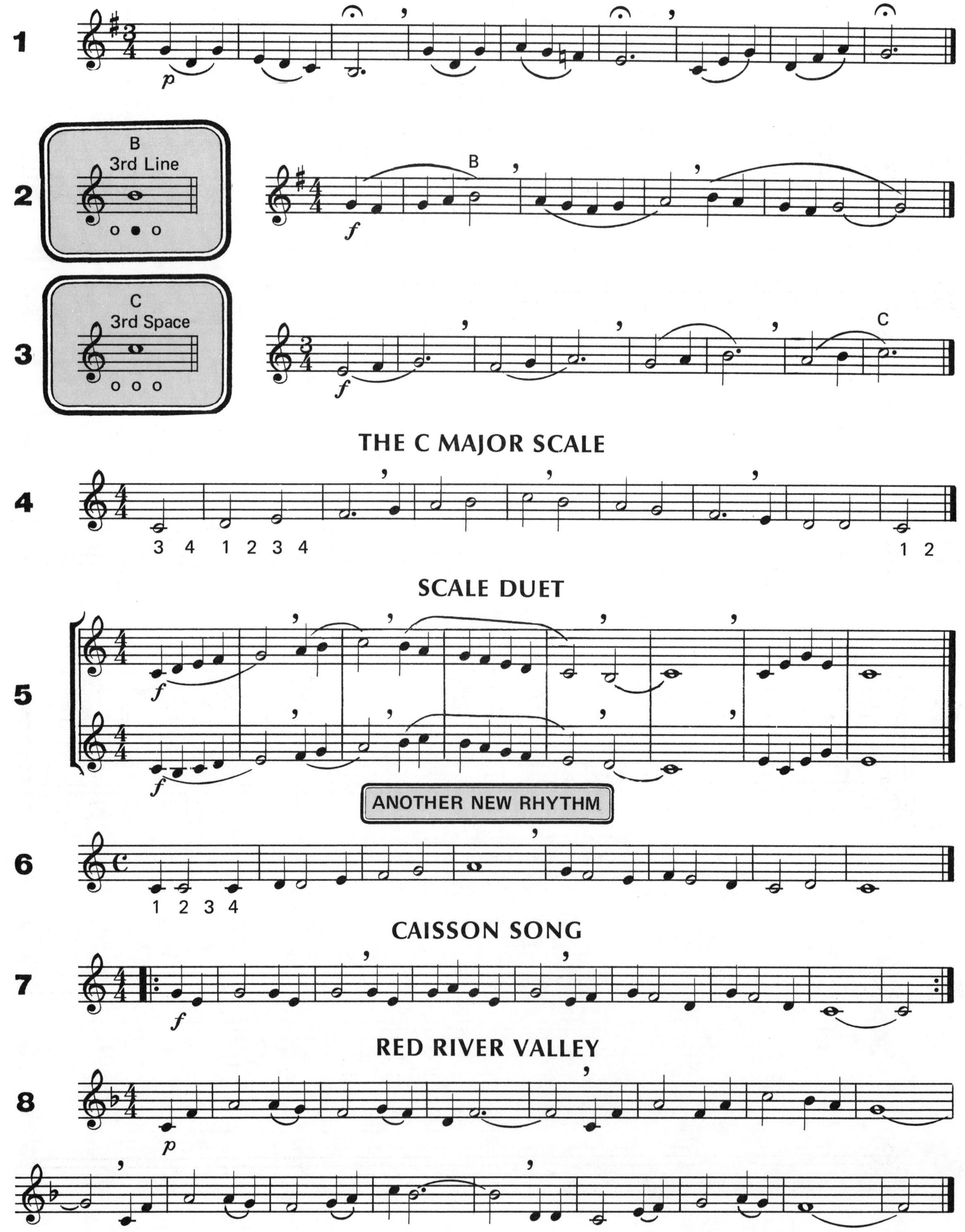

SCALE WITH CHROMATICS

9

Name all the notes in this exercise.

> The <u>Accent</u> (>) means the <u>attack</u> should be more forceful than normal.

10

Do you recognize the melody in the accented notes?

MORE INTERVALS

11

ARTICULATION

12

RHYTHM DUET

13

SCOTLAND'S BURNING
(Round)

14

> ℀ means to repeat the previous measure.

CHROMATICS IN F MAJOR

15

UNIT 9

WARM-UP

DOXOLOGY

DOXOLOGY
7
THE VOLGA BOATMAN
Russian folk song
8
MEXICAN HAT DANCE
Mexican folk song
9
1.
2.
INTERVAL STUDY
10
CHROMATICS IN G MAJOR
11
Name all the notes in this exercise.
12
OCTAVE ETUDE
13

UNIT 10

REVIEW AND SUPPLEMENTARY STUDIES

SCALES

1 C Major

2 F Major

3 G Major

4 D Major

LIP SLURS

5

6

7

CHROMATICS

8

9

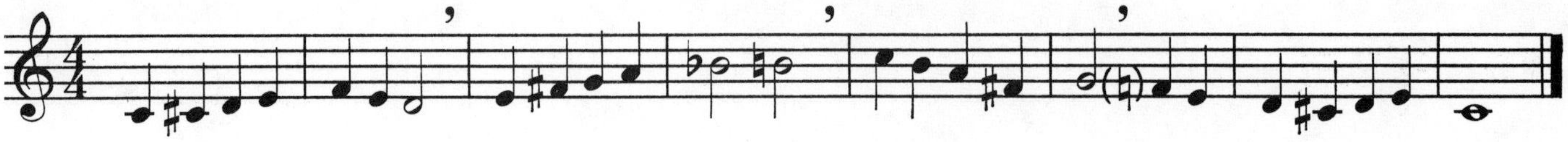

SCALE THIRDS

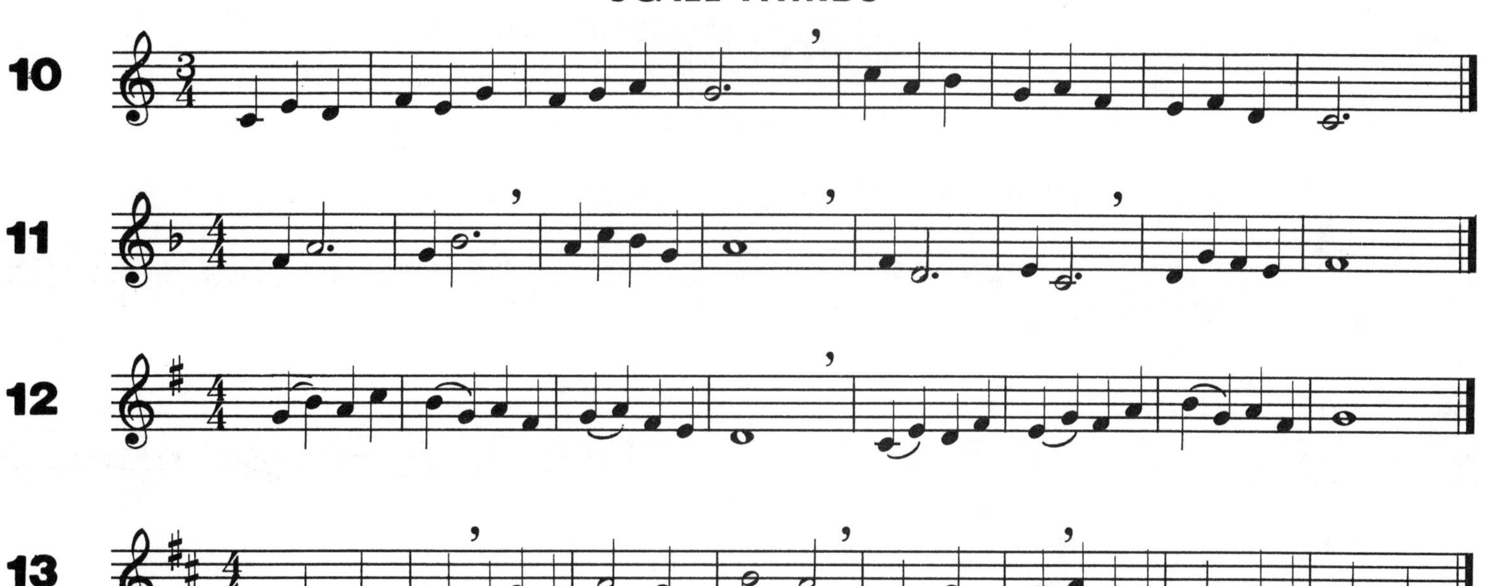

INTERVALS

ARPEGGIOS

BAND UNIT A

WHOLE NOTES AND WHOLE RESTS

HALF NOTES AND HALF RESTS
1
1 2 3 4
1 2 3 4
Group 2
2
2
3
COMMON TIME
4
1 2 3 4
1 2 3 4
2
1.
2.
5
LITTLE SCHERZO
2
6
DRUM FESTIVAL
7
LAND OF THE RISING SUN
2
8
JUBILEE
2
1.
2.
9
FREEWAY
2
10

BAND UNIT C

WARM-UP
D
C
REST STOP
Bb
Group 2
AMERICAN FOLK TUNE
MERRILY WE ROLL ALONG
LITTLE BAND BLUES

BAND UNIT D

Group 2
WARM-UP
WALTZ WITH RESTS
RETURN TO "GO"
F#
Fine
D.C. al Fine
SKIPS
ECHOS
LONDON BRIDGE
POP GOES THE WEASEL

BAND UNIT E

Group 2
WARM-UP
Fine
D.C. al Fine
CHROMATICS
LIGHTLY ROW
BEAUTIFUL BROWN EYES

BAND UNIT F

Group 2
WARM-UP
1
A FAMILIAR MELODY WITH SKIPS
2
1.
2.
PICK-ME-UP
3
4 1 2 3 4
1 2 3
ROUND ABOUT
(Round)
1
2
4
5
6
1.
2.
BELLS
7
f
Fine
D.C. al Fine
8
f
p
Beethoven
ODE TO JOY
9
1.
2.
f
Rest 1st time
Play 2nd time only
ORIENTAL EXPRESS
10

BAND UNIT G

WARM-UP
Group 2
B
1
REST ON 1
2
1 2 3 4
1.,
2.,
INTERVALS
2
3
A NEW RHYTHM WITH TIES
4
p
Wait until the 2nd beat.
INCH WORM
3
5
p
2
6
ANOTHER NEW RHYTHM
7
1 2 3 4
CAISSON SONG
2
8
3 4 1 2 3 4
f
1 2
PLYMOUTH ROCK
1
9

BAND UNIT H

Group 2
WARM-UP
TWO MELODIES
ROUND HOUSE
(Round)
SCALE WITH A BEAT
MEXICAN JUMPING BEAN
LITTLE BROWN JUG
CARNIVAL

BAND UNIT I

WARM-UP

ROCK TIME

I.

Group 1

BIG BEN VARIATIONS

RONDO

WE'LL RANT AND WE'LL ROAR

*Return to Sign ( ) and play to *Fine.*

OVERTURA

CHRISTMAS SUITE

I. Jolly Old St. Nicholas

II. We Three Kings

III. Jingle Bells

NOTES